PRAISE FOR *G.O.S.P.E.L.*

One of the most misunderstood doctrines in the urban context is the Gospel. D.A. not only highlights how essential the Gospel is, but clearly articulates and defines the Gospel for the often forgotten and misunderstood urban culture.

> LECRAE
> *Reach Records artist of bestselling album* Rehab

G.O.S.P.E.L. isn't breaking ground but it is groundbreaking. Having a Latino urban theological voice on the issue of the Gospel is a profound need. With this work Pastor Horton helps to bring the simple (not simplistic) solution of the Gospel to a complex urban context.

> ERIC MASON
> *Lead Pastor of Epiphany Fellowship, Philadelphia*

Damon Horton is a young pastor with a passion to communicate the gospel in a relevant format to the urban sector in such a way that they can receive the message, comprehend the message, and apply the message to their lives. This book takes the theological issues that are often overlooked or ignored and drives home the meaning of the Gospel with clarity. Reverend Horton has answered the question well, "What is the Gospel?"

> JAMES L. CLARK, PhD
> *President of Calvary Bible College and Theological Seminary*

There are few who can preach to the thug on the street corner as well as the seminary student in the lecture hall. Damon does both, and does it effectively. The diversity of people in his church is living proof. Even though we minister in different cities, our passion is the same: to spread the seed of the Gospel in the soil of broken communities.

> BRIAN DYE
> *Pastor of Legacy Fellowship, Chicago*

D.A. Horton is a gifted preacher and poet who has addressed the most important category in Scripture—that is the Gospel. D.A. tackles the Gospel with insightful "thebonics" as he proclaims Christ to both the urban and suburban street. I predict D.A. will continue to impact lives for the glory of Christ as long as the cross continues to be central in all he does.

> JEREMY KRAUSE
> *Student Ministries Pastor*
> *First Evangelical Free Church, Wichita, Kansas*

D. A. Horton has provided a practical and accessible tool that will prove to be exceedingly helpful for the inner-city context. This book clearly communicates the truths of the Gospel in a way that the "Block" can grab hold. This book puts Jesus on display, and it has a great balance of practice and theology. Read it, use it, and teach it often!

> DOUG LOGAN, JR.
> *Lead Pastor, Epiphany Fellowship of Camden, New Jersey*

Damon addresses an issue that hits home to the church, both in the "burbs" and the "hood." He gives us the heart of the Gospel with clarity and a solid biblical foundation. After nearly thirty years of ministry and countless mission trips with both students and adults, I am happy to endorse a handbook on how to share the Gospel in any context. His presentation shows that the Gospel transcends time and cultures with the power of the love of Christ.

> GEOFF SAFFORD
> *Celebration Lead, Westwind Church*

D. A. Horton's knowledge of the Word, his love for his family, and his care for God's people make him a sharp tool in God's hand. His contribution to the urban community is groundbreaking. Listen to him, learn from him, and experience his leadership.

> FLAME
> *Artist of chart-topping album* Captured

G.O.S.P.E.L.

D. A. HORTON

MOODY PUBLISHERS
CHICAGO

Scripture taken from The New King James Version. Copyright © 1982,
1992 by Thomas Nelson, Inc. Used by permission. All rights reserved.

Lyrics to raps songs at the end of chapters 2–7 are from the CD
"GOSPEL" and reprinted by permission of the author. Copyright ©
2012 by D. A. Horton.

Edited by Jim Vincent
Interior design: Smartt Guys design
Cover design: Brent Rice
Cover image: Courtesy of Deviant Art and Brent Rice
Author photo: Filip Blank

978-0-8024-0589-0

We hope you enjoy this book from Moody Publishers. Our goal is
to provide high-quality, thought-provoking books and products that
connect truth to your real needs and challenges. For more information on other books and products written and produced from a biblical perspective, go to
www.moodypublishers.com
or write to:

Moody Publishers
820 N. LaSalle Boulevard
Chicago, IL 60610

3 5 7 9 10 8 6 4 2

Printed in the United States of America

But even if our gospel is veiled, it is veiled to those who are perishing, whose minds the god of this age has blinded, who do not believe, lest the light of the gospel of the glory of Christ, who is the image of God, should shine on them.
(2 Corinthians 4:3–4)

Contents

The Gospel for Our Cities

The Lord has blessed me with opportunities to travel to cities across our nation to preach, teach, and rap about Jesus Christ. No matter where I travel, I'm always asked one of two questions: When in the hood, "What is the Gospel?" and when in the suburbs, "How can I present the Gospel in a way that is nonoffensive to people living in an urban setting?"

The first question will be answered later in this book. Before we answer the second question, I must qualify the term "nonoffensive." Contrary to what you may be thinking, "nonoffensive" does not pertain to the offense of the cross Paul writes about in Galatians 5:11, as the cross strips away all human merit and work toward earning salvation. The "offense" is the fear of suburban saints saying something that culturally offends minorities in the areas of race, social status, or stereotype that will give minorities a reason to be turned off from receiving the Gospel. This fear holds many saints hostage as they remain stagnant and distant from presenting the Gospel to minorities.

They believe their only option to seeing the Great Commission fulfilled in the inner city is the ministry of intercessory prayer, asking God to send someone other than them to reach urban minorities.

Due to gentrification—the moving of young professionals into the cities—many suburb-dwelling Christians are seeing more of the urban population moving into their communities and churches. So many of the urban issues, such as racial tensions, noticeable gang activity, poverty, and a spike in violent crime, are now present in the area where they have done ministry for years. The urban mission field that was once a world away, even though within a short twenty-minute drive, is now an immediate reality.

FOUR POINTS OF ACTION

This reality forces the suburban church to contemplate new ways of presenting the Gospel to a population they think they cannot sympathize with. For my brothers and sisters whose culture is not one that is privy to an urban *swag*, I want to encourage you to no longer allow yourselves to be paralyzed by fearing the *what ifs* that mentally bombard you when God places urban missions on your heart or in your context. My encouragement is bathed with intentional prayers that you would receive comfort by four brief, but key action steps the Lord has placed on my heart. As you gain full confidence in Christ when engaged with the urban context, these truths will be a backbone in boldly sharing the Gospel in an uncomfortable missional setting.

(By the way, if you can't figure what *swag* means in the previous paragraph and why it's shown in boldface and italics, look at the Thebonics glossary at the end of this book. *Thebonics* is the presentation of theological truths in the language known as Ebonics, the rich slang that is part of our urban neighborhoods, especially African-American, to describe people and situations in the hood. All words in bold italics appear in the glossary. For more on Thebonics and the glossary, see Action Step #4.)

Action Step #1: *Focus on the Gospel, which transcends all cultures.* The apostle Paul informs us in Romans 1:16–17 that he has no shame in presenting the Gospel to either Jew or Gentile, for the simple fact that the Gospel is "the power of God to salvation" to both groups. It is the Gospel that carries the omnipotent power of God to regenerate the sinner, not our method of presentation. The Gospel alone that confronts sinners with the reality that they, like us, deserve eternal punishment for sin. The Gospel alone exposes both saint and sinner to the righteousness of God. Lastly, we must remember that the Gospel is the only message reaching sinners from every race, subculture, and socioeconomic class. The phrase "from faith to faith" highlights the truth that each individual person who has ever been saved, is being saved, and will be saved was brought to faith in Christ by the proclamation of the Gospel.

Be encouraged; the Gospel does not weaken because of the presenter's skin color, background, or preference in style of music. If you wrestle with this, please reread John 3:3–8 and let it take this pressure off your back. We must remember that God the Holy Spirit is responsible for bringing *regeneration* to the sinner, not the church or our methods. Minorities in the inner city are in need of the same Gospel that is preached to the white-collar CEO in the suburbs. It is the message of the Gospel that contains power, so with boldness, preach the Gospel and leave the rest to God and He will work out His plan of redemption in the life of the hearer!

Action Step #2: *Get to know the culture of the city.* I challenge you to invest time conducting research on trends in the areas of social issues and entertainment that thrive in your local inner city. A plethora of websites will allow you to perform demographic studies to discover up-to-date statistics on the area God is calling you to target. In addition, plan to go out in groups into the community you have a heart for and talk to the people living there. Some of the best conversations I've had with urban dwellers were located in one of two locations: the barbershop and the bus stop. The barbershop is to the city what the coffee shop is to the suburbs—a place of meeting, for business and community. The bus stop or the street corner (also affectionately known as *the block*) is a place where the differing philosophies of life, politics, and religion are often discussed in the open. (It should go without saying that business deals are made here regularly as well.) A biblical parallel for the corner gatherings in the hood would be the "city gates" we read of in Scripture.

As you spend time in these places, I challenge you to assess your findings and document your research in a journal so you can reference specific people, places, and situations. This will be extremely helpful as you pray for the inner city or begin discipling new believers. You can and should know the culture of those living in the city.

I also challenge you to ask the Lord to give you ideas, discernment, and compassion for the saved and the lost in the community, and that He would plant more Gospel-centered churches in the inner city that will serve as beacons of light amidst the darkness.

Action Step #3: *Demonstrate authenticity.* There is no need for you to act as if you personify the urban swag if you can't identify with it. Don't pretend to be what you are not. Rather, focus on what you and the urbanite have in common: your struggle and fall into sin and your need of a Savior. Don't try to act *hood*. Instead, just focus on God's command for holiness.

In addition, there is no reason to force slang initially. As you grow in relationship with people, you will learn what boundaries you have regarding conversation with them individually. So when you first begin to lay the foundations for fellowship, focus on the Scriptures, and don't force slang.

Lastly, don't try to "dress the part" by urbanizing your wardrobe. Urbanites, socially speaking, have a keen sense of discernment and can spot a stranger who is fake a mile away.

I challenge you to be authentic with your dress and personality; you are not acting in a play but rather you are an ambassador for Christ. Seek to represent Him well so that your actions or dress won't distract sinners from the cross.

Action Step #4: *Study the Thebonical glossary.* The final element of encouragement that I can offer you is a condensed glossary of terms of what I call *Thebonics*. Ebonics derives from ebony and phonics (street slang), and theology derives from the Greek word *theos*, which means "God," and *ology* from the Greek *logia*, meaning "to study or speak of." Thebonics is the merging of theological truths rendered in Scripture and broken down into bite-size pieces to be exposited to the urban context in its own unique language of Ebonics.

As with every dialect, trends and definitions vary from region to region, thus the reason for the condensed Thebonical glossary versus that which is exhaustive. Rhetoricians call such slang *Ebonics*. Thebonics melds Ebonics with theological terms to help those from the inner city better understand the meaning of the Gospel. Go ahead, look up *swag* now, and while there look up a nearby theological word, like *remission*.

HIP HOP IN ACTION

As part of the suburban church looking for new ways of presenting the Gospel to a population you know little about, you do your homework, learning about the culture (Step #2) and acting authentic (Step #3). There are many ways to do both of these, but one I will introduce in this book involves knowing the music. The sounds of the city can form a powerful communication bridge.

Growing up in the inner city positioned me in the heart of a subculture known as "hip hop." Within the four widely recognized elements of hip hop (DJ'ing, Emceein', Graffiti, and Breakin'), the most vocal element is the musical genre known as rap (Emceein'). Rap's humble beginnings identified itself as an urban artistic and poetic expression centered on the social issues the dominant culture of America failed to address. So becoming familiar with rap is a key way to learn about the strains and pain of city life.

Within a short span of twenty-plus years, rap has morphed into an accepted, worldwide vehicle of communication, commercialism, and controversy. Most onlookers of the hip-hop culture are unaware of how rap music acts as a tool of education. In the late eighties emcees (rappers) were using rap as a caveat of didactic instruction on topics ranging from diets and nutrition to the dogma of the Nation of Gods and Earths (5%ers).[1] In the nineties the majority of education through lyrical content was marginalized, with topics including cooking crack and the glorification of sexual exploits. Sadly to date, the state of rap lyrics for the most part has quickly declined further.

A few years ago I stepped back to examine the genre of rap from a biblical worldview. I wondered what it would look like to merge Bible-centered didactic instruction with beats and rhymes. In June of 2010 I independently released *Systematic Theology Volume One*, the first of four CDs that would merge systematic theology with rap. (This CD can be purchased on iTunes.) *Systematic Theology Volume One* was well received by pastors, seminary professors, and young people alike. The only push back I received was a request: "Can you do something more evangelistic to reach the lost through rap, so that we could then introduce them to your systematic theology projects for discipleship?"

I received this feedback while working on the *GOSPEL* book and sensed the Lord leading me to write "lyrical versions" of each chapter. The lyrics that end each of the first seven chapters are to help you and me hear the culture speak through songs on the "GOSPEL."[2] (Some terms in the Thebonics glossary appear in a couple of the rap songs.)

GOSPEL and the CD "GOSPEL"[2] were both written and produced to be tools for evangelism. They are in harmony with God's Word and are designed to benefit individuals and local churches in reaching the lost in our cities. (The CD includes instrumental versions of each song that can be used by anyone in the local church to perform before congregations and communities for the glory of God by advancing His Gospel message.) I urge you to read through these lyrics and to realize that rap music is simply one method of evangelism. Yet this *method*, like all others, is powerless when it does not include the *message* of the Gospel.

On a personal note, as you read this book, please keep in mind that God has privileged me to be saved out of the streets, and it was He alone who set me apart. He allowed me to be seasoned with a biblical education so that I would be prepared to go back to the streets sent as a missionary. It's my desire to share with you a glimpse of the mission field I love that is often overlooked in our country. Many churches that have both influence and resources focus mainly on "across the seas" missions while neglecting "across the street" missions. My heart is to have more saints who know the Gospel and possess a heart's grief for the lost to become engaged in urban mission work here in America, both in the inner city and the suburbs.

The first step in seeing the Great Commission succeed in the urban core is preaching the Gospel in a way that is contextual and relevant to the unique issues in the urban context. This book is but a frail attempt at jump-starting your passion for preaching the Gospel to "my people."

NOTES

1. In 1969 "the Father" Clarence 13X founded The Nation of Gods and Earths in Harlem, New York. This urban cultural movement teaches that the world's population fell into three groups. The great majority, 85 percent, were ignorant that the Original Man (any ethnicity found in the sixteen shades of black) is god. Another 10 percent, like leeches, live off the 85 percent. Only the "5%ers" are classified as the Poor Righteous Teachers, who through the teachings of the "lessons," can bring truth to the "85%ers." Today many popular rappers, including Rakim Allah, the Wu Tang Clan, and Poor Righteous Teachers, use hip-hop life and culture as a means of evangelism for their Nation.

2. The downloadable CD "Gospel" is available on iTunes beginning in mid-January 2012.

1

The Need for the Gospel

Recently I was asked to minister, through preaching and Gospel-centered rap, to a group of teens from the south side of Kansas City's urban core. Toward the end of my sermon, I asked how many of them had been saved by Jesus. Immediately, with all confidence, forty-plus hands were thrown up as if I just asked who wanted free money. Their response led to my second question, *What is the Gospel?* Their hands went down just as quickly as they rose, and puzzled looks of confusion began to cover every face in the auditorium.

Keeping their attention, I immediately asked how long each of them had been in church and how long they have been **saved.** Students at once began to shout out, "I've been in church and saved since I was born," and "I've been saved since I was two, and that's when I started coming to church." As the conversation picked up momentum, a change took place that was evident by the puzzled looks that jumped off their faces and onto mine, making room for them to **rock** a confidence that would humble

Kanye West.

As my heart grieved, I silently asked God to help me bring clarity to these precious young people by providing me with an illustration to share with them that would hit home. To God's glory, He answered my prayer immediately. As the students sat there assured of themselves, I asked them a question that would begin to expose the harsh reality they were failing to see. I gripped the microphone tightly, brought it close to my lips, and asked, "How long has Young Money been around?" With continued confidence, the students shouted, "two to two-and-a-half-years." I then asked the students to name all the rappers on Young Money, and with joy students began to look at each other with competition in their eyes. Each student tried to outshout everyone else in the auditorium with the names of rappers on Young Money, such as Lil Wayne, Drake, Nicki Minaj, Cory Gunz, Gudda Gudda, Jae Mills, Lil Chuckee, and Lil Twist.

Their ability to quickly rattle off so many names prompted me to step in and make my point. I put the microphone back up to my lips. "Okay, okay, *I see you,*" and the students all began to laugh. However, their laughter soon turned to embarrassment as I gently exposed them to the reality they failed to see. I quieted them down and broke the silence by softly saying, "You mean to tell me that you all claim to know Jesus as your Savior, you have been in church for all of your lives, and you cannot tell me the one message God has declared to be the power of salvation to the sinner—yet you can rattle off every rapper on Young Money who has only been out for a few years?" A hush of disbelief fell on everyone in the room!

Two weeks later I was privileged to minister through preaching and Gospel-centered rap at a fall conference for youth from a solid suburban church in the Minneapolis metropolitan area. When asked if they knew the Gospel, their response was the exact opposite of the urban youth. Most of them were able to communicate the Gospel, and it was at this point I realized the problem: the urban students could not communicate the Gospel because they did not understand the Gospel, even though they belong to a church that faithfully preaches the Gospel. I know both youth pastors personally, and know they communicate the Gospel to their youth, yet the suburban church has a greater success rate than the urban church when it comes to students actually knowing and **spillin'** the Gospel.

This begs the question: Why?

I didn't realize it at the time, but a young, urban, teenage girl at the Kansas City event answered my question when she bluntly said, "Tonight when you preached the message, it was the first time I ever understood what Jesus did for me. Thank you!" The message I shared that night was broken down into bite-size pieces with illustrations to which urban students could relate. The message I shared that night was the GOSPEL, the six-part message of good news that follows in chapters 2–7.

A GOSPEL Rap

"THE NEED"

Hook:

My whole life has been unfair / I go thru the motions but am not there
Life's passed by, I'm so distant / I want to stop existing and
    finally start living.

You said I could go to you. How can I get close to you?
What am I supposed to do—to believe in what I know is true?
Please tell me what I need, tell me, tell me, tell me what I need. (2x)

Verse 1:

I'ma put you up on game, show you yo deficiency.
I know that you wanna change, from the hopeless misery.
I know that you cope with pain, drinking Coke & Hennessey,
And smoking thangs that blow ya brain, if that's you, yo come
    get wit me.

What I got's not what ya want, but I know it's what you need.
The Gospel is yo medicine, prescription for yo disease—
A disease that we all had since our conception.
The Gospel message "Ushers" in "these are my confessions."

I'm open air yellin', wake up this life ain't "just a dream"
That ends with frostbite, from all of our custom bling.
Salvation's call's God's VIP custom ring
That will have ya screaming "OMG" like when "Usher" sings.

Verse 2:

You would think that in the church all our people got it all,

Not all, when the Gospel's defined as the altar call.

Somebody tell these pastors ain't nut'n funny

When our kids despise Christ, but idolize Young Money.

Our Kids praise grills, chase thrills, takin' pain pills

Shorty, the Gospel is the flood warnin', Jae Mills.

The Gospel's an offense, it murders yo' feelings

So God will blow the roof off ya dome, no ceilings.

I used to live a life darker than whisky in bars

Then the Light of Christ shined right thru me, Nicki Minaj.

I spit the Gospel to the elderly and lil kids;

It's the best kept "little secret" wit a "lil twist."

Verse 3:

Ya pain is so intense ya cut yaself to relieve hurt

Ya searched for joy, can't find it, look again, . . . research.

Christ went to the cross for our joy's sake,

So we'd never be "so far gone" like that boy Drake.

He took the punishment for all ya sin, like He did it

Forgiveness He wit it, accept Him wit Glee like Eve—get it?

I just gave ya the Gospel, can ya dig now?

Get a life & chuck ya deuces to the world, Chris Brown.

2

G—God's Image

All of us have asked the questions "Why am I here?" and "Does my life really mean anything?" Every day we look to people, places, and things other than God to answer these questions because we feel like God is so far away from us. He seems so far away from our struggles and from our pain that He can't answer us, and even if He did, how could we hear Him through all the sirens, screaming, gunshots, and trunk-rattling bass?

The truth that we fail to realize daily is that God understands the struggles we face because He is the one who created us. When God created the first man, Adam, He made him in His image. Let's *chop it up* about the creation of Adam for a second. The first thing you need to realize is that he was the physical father of all humans on the planet who have ever lived, are living, and will ever live. When God created Adam, He gave him certain characteristics that He didn't give to any other type of creation, such as animals, insects, plants, all of nature, and everything else in the universe.

Genesis 1:26–27 says, "Then God said, 'Let Us make man in Our image, according to Our likeness; let them have dominion over the fish of the sea, over the birds of the air, and over the cattle, over all the earth and over every creeping thing that creeps on the earth.' So God created man in His own image; in the image of God He created him; male and female He created them."

The word *image* in this Scripture does not speak of a physical image or a body, but rather the nonphysical qualities that God chose to give only to humans, with limitations. Some of these qualities include emotions that are displayed through our personalities, the ability to make reasonable decisions, a basic knowledge of right from wrong, and a living spirit. John 4:24 tells us, "God is Spirit, and those who worship Him must worship in spirit and truth." This Scripture **puts us up on game** to the fact that not only is God a spirit without a physical body,[1] but that humans have been given the desire and ability to worship God because we have been given a spirit like His.

This is the perfect time to explain how God put limitations on the qualities He gave us, and we'll use the example of our spirit. The Bible clearly tells us in Genesis 1:1, "In the beginning God created," proving that God is not a created being and He demonstrated this to us by creating all of creation. God created us; we were made in the image of God, meaning He gave us a spirit that began to exist when we were conceived in our mother's womb, and our spirit will continue to exist after our flesh dies. Even though we will continue to exist after death, we are not like God because we are limited by having a starting point to our life, and God does not because He has always existed. This is often overlooked because many people don't take the time to understand the biblical meaning of being made in the image of God.

When we try to make the word *image* in Genesis 1:26–27 mean a physical body, we buy into the lie that humans are either equal with God, or are a lower-class of gods, because we are His **replicas**. It's kind of like **rockin'** a jersey of your favorite sports team. Since I'm a Kansas City Chiefs fan—**don't hate**—I often show love for my Chiefs by wearing either my **throwback** jersey or my replica jersey. But **real talk**, even if I rock an authentic throwback jersey with the letters "Dawson" stitched on the back, or if I rock a modern replica jersey with "Johnson" on the back, is that neither jersey can transform me into Hall of Fame Quarterback Len Dawson or Pro-Bowl Linebacker Derrick Johnson. Rockin' a jersey only shows that I'm representing the team I love and the players I respect, not replicating them.

In a similar way, being made in the image of God does not mean that we are equal with God or even His little clones. Rather, each day as we live, rockin' the image of God, we have the opportunity to represent Him by following His command of reproducing and ruling that's found in Genesis 2.

Before we move on, let's recap. God created man in His image so that man could represent Him by reproducing and ruling over creation. Being created in God's image does not make man a god any more than rocking a throwback makes me a professional football player. Now that we got this point straight, let's move on to the next one.

NOTE

1.   We will deal with God the Son putting on flesh like an outfit to pay the price for sin in chapter 6.

A GOSPEL Rap

"GOD'S IMAGE"

Hook: We was made for representin' Him (3x)—Are ya
   representin Him? (I represent, I represent)

Verse 1

I know You be like . . .
Can God know my struggle (know my struggle)?
Can He feel my pain (feel my pain)?
If I was born to hustle, Tell me, how I run a differ'nt lane?
This is all I know . . . All I know is I'ma do me,
Straight grind, take mine, Spray nines and Uzis.

I be like . . .
Yea, He knows ya struggle (knows ya struggle) and knows ya
   pain (knows ya pain).
[He]created you for a purpose, God even knows ya name.
Made in His image, hold up let me set it straight.
[we were] Made for representin' Him; don't try to replicate.

We ain't God, even tho we made in God's image.

He's infinite, we finite, meaning that we got limits.

He shared with us some of His qualities; know that

Daily we rock these qualities like a throwback.

Verse 2

I know You be like . . .

If I was made by God . . . . tell me where all my power is!

Every time I wanna do right, it's like I'm powerless.

Now I just keep fallin' and I don't even care no mo (more)

[there's] Too many strikes against me, I can't even bear no mo
   (more).

I be like . . .

Just like you know the bass in this beat is nice and strong,

God put inside us [the ability] to know right from wrong.

He gave us the desire to get to know Him;

Problem is that our sin separates us and we don't know Him.

We was made to obey and be producers, not consumers.

Sin is serious, our ***Kevin Hart's*** mock in humor;

But when we're wronged, we seek revenge like Montezuma

Then surround ourselves with those who give us praise like
   "Hallelujah."

Verse 3

I Know You be like . . .

Tell me who is God, tell me why was I born here.

Tell me why I got scars and why my heart is torn here.

If He do exist, tell me why I always feel alone?

Do He know I got hate in my heart that's deep like a Killa's jones?

I be like . . .

God is Father, God the Son, and God Holy Spirit

Acts 17 He made you in a placed to get to know these lyrics.

You bear the scars of sin in ya life from top to bottom

But God is sovereign, He alone can absolve them.

Real talk He exists, it's ya sin that's separating Him

You can't relate to Him, because ya heart relates to sin!

You know ya hate within, and yes it's blatant sin,

He can forgive it, Christ died in ya place for sin.

3

O—Open Fellowship

Genesis 2:7–25 gives us more detail about the creation of man and his automatic *fellowship* with God. *Fellowship* is another word that describes a relationship to someone or something. It carries the idea of being connected to someone because of what we have in common.

On the streets, when cats are seriously *movin' weight*, unless they are *smugglin'* in their product themselves, they are connected to suppliers who provide them with product to sell. Dealers will have the benefit of being supplied with product as long as they keep to the laws suppliers normally hit them off with: move the product, and if a dealer ever gets *pinched*, he/she is to never rat out the supplier. The supplier and dealer are connected with the common interest of making money, which is what brought them together in fellowship. If the dealer breaks just one of these laws the supplier has set up, the result will normally end in the death of the dealer.

Such fellowship among drug traffickers makes us

wince, mainly because the city—like the suburbs and now even rural areas of many states—has criminals who form their camarderie based on breaking civil laws and God's law. In contrast, we read that in the beginning everything God created was good, meaning there was no evil present in the world (Genesis 1:31). It's hard to imagine, but it's the reality of how holy God is. Since Adam was created by God, he too was without sin and had no knowledge of wrongdoing.

The easiest way to describe sin is simply breaking God's law. Adam and Eve were both connected to God and would remain connected as long as they both obeyed the laws God gave them for their good. In Genesis 1–2, God clearly outlines the law for Adam to obey: be fruitful and multiply, tend the garden of Eden, and eat fruit from any tree except the Tree of Knowledge of Good and Evil.

Sounds simple, right? As long as Adam and Eve obeyed God's laws, they would enjoy open fellowship and remain connected to God. However, if one or both of them broke God's laws, their fellowship with God would be closed and their loss of access to a supply of spiritual life would start a countdown to their physical death. So the common interest that God, Adam, and Eve all shared was the reality that the created man and woman were not guilty of breaking any laws and were, at that time, without sin. Therefore they had open fellowship with God, the Creator.

As mentioned in the previous chapter, Adam was

commanded to represent God by reproducing and ruling over creation. God provided Adam with everything he needed to reproduce: He placed Adam in a garden that God planted (He provided a job for him); He gave Adam instructions on how to be good at his job (He provided on-the-job training); and He gave Adam a special gift, a wife. Now Adam and Eve could reproduce humans and fill the earth, and all humans could have open fellowship with God and represent Him all over the earth as they obeyed the commandments of God.

Adam was commanded to rule over creation, which included ruling over Eve. To *rule* in this passage meant to manage, not abuse, so man was never created to abuse a woman in any way. So the question you are probably asking is, "How was Adam supposed to rule over Eve?" Simply put, he was to provide for her in two specific ways: in fellowship and education.

Fellowship. The first time in all of Scripture that God said something was not good is when man was without someone who was of his kind (see Genesis 2:18). All other species on the planet had another of their kind except Adam, so God blessed him by giving him a wife whom he could have fellowship with just as God the Father, God the Son, and God the Holy Spirit have always had fellowship with each other.

Education. Just as Adam received education from God regarding His laws, Adam was to educate Eve on how to maintain open fellowship with God. Genesis 2 shows us that in the beginning of humanity, all things were on point regarding knowledge on how to stay in open fellowship with God.

In Genesis 2:25 we read that Adam and Eve were naked and had no shame. The phrase *not ashamed* in this passage means to not have a fear of being exposed. Can you imagine life with no **baby mama** or **baby daddy drama**? Now imagine having open fellowship with someone to the point that you don't have to watch your back around this person, and you can fully trust the person because there are no skeletons in the closet to keep hiding. This is exactly what Adam and Eve had twenty-four hours a day—not just with each other but with God! God had open fellowship with both Adam and Eve because they all had something in common: none of them were stained by sin! Adam obeyed God by following His commands, and by the time we arrive at Genesis 3, we see that Adam had already **hit off** Eve with the teaching he received from God because she quoted the commands of God to the serpent.

Let's recap before we move on to the next point. When God created Adam and Eve, they were both without sin and had open fellowship or "connection" to God as their supplier of life. God gave Adam the laws he needed to follow in order to remain connected in open fellowship. Through Genesis 2, all things were on point! Now that we have this nailed down, let's move on to the next point.

A GOSPEL Rap

"OPEN FELLOWSHIP"

Verse 1

Let me breathe, sigh of relief, we open.

Skeleton key to my heart, I'm devoted.

Every closet clean, no need to keep probin'.

Short-E got the best of my love—Emotions.

Password to the email, Facebook, Myspace's our space,

Every tweet, she knows it.

Communion without elements a priest holdin'

We 2 eye to eye like numerals that be Roman.

Peace hope and . . . love we share daily,

Kind of like loaf of bread wit a piece broken.

I know it's kind of hard to fathom, like deep oceans (get it?)

This is life wit God as ya center, keep posted.

Our relationship ain't perfect, we got baggage.

From the jump, Adam and Eve didn't have this.

A perfect world they forfeited, matchless;

Now thru conflict we gotta cling to Christ not magic.

Verse 2

So what up boo, let me get ya "open" like a Sun roof.

Put ya on game on how I always come thru.

Wit no Bon Qui Qui, "I'll cut you,"

Because I love you and I trust you.

Indeed life wit me's a breeze, no drama.

Trust I'm not a 2, 3, or 4 timer!

I provide my Bride wit more Hope than Obama.

It's me u shoulda "been laudin" (Bin Laden), Osama (get it)?

Because sin is no joke, like yo mamma,

I judged my Son in ya place, for yo honor.

Hand to God the Holy Spirit's my Co-signer.

You're a diamond in the ruff, I'm ya Coal Miner.

Let's get it open, clean out ya closet.

Come to Christ & I'll overlook ya past, *Cuz*, the cross kid.

I mend broken hearts wit, wit, wit, with my Cross-stitch.

Obedience Provides Eternal Nearness, acrostic.

4

S—Sin Introduced

In chapter 3, we used the illustration of a drug dealer remaining connected to his supplier as long as the dealer doesn't break the two laws a supplier normally sets up. When either of these laws are broken, the penalty is almost always death.

I've had friends who got pinched, spent a few hours or days in jail only to be released, even though they were busted with a sizable amount of *weight* on them. On the streets, it is common knowledge in the dope game that when this happens, it's probably because the dealer snitched and passed the blame onto someone else in order to walk. So when the dealer gets out, word already got back to his supplier that he probably snitched—and the next time the dealer is seen is usually on the ten o'clock news when the body is found.

In Genesis 3, the story takes a turn for the worse as Adam and Eve disobey God by breaking His law. As a result of their disobedience, the Bible teaches us that death entered the world for the first time—two deaths, to be exact: one that is physical and one that is spiritual.

The best way to define death is not by saying someone no longer exists, because earlier we discussed how our soul lives on after our body has died. **Death** is simply being separated from that which sustains life. Physical death is separation from oxygen or something else that is required to live. Spiritual death is separation from God, who is Spirit.

After Adam and Eve broke God's law, they went on the run—Bonnie and Clyde style—to hide from God. For the first time in their lives, they were ashamed and realized they were naked, which showed they had lost the nothing-to-hide purity they once possessed. When God confronted Adam, he passed the blame on to his wife and failed to man up for his own mistake. The realness of what took place when Adam and Eve sinned is the fact that their open fellowship with God ended. This resulted in them being cut off from God, their supplier of life. Now they were spiritually dead!

In the dope game, a supplier kills the dealer because the supplier knows by allowing the dealer to live there's the probability of the supplier getting pinched. In the war on drugs, taking down a general of a **cartel** is much more newsworthy than busting a nickel-and-dime-bag pusher. This is where we have to leave the illustration of the dope game to focus on God's reason for cutting off Adam and Eve from fellowship. The reason God had to separate Himself from Adam and Eve was because He is holy, meaning not only is He without sin, but He can't fellowship with anyone who has been stained by sin.

In Leviticus 11:44, God commands His people to "be holy; for I am holy." This is a command, not a suggestion. Yet sin is in us and precedes us, all the way back to Adam. In Romans 5:12, the Bible tells us when Adam sinned, death entered into the world and has remained here since. Adam is the physical father of us all; when he sinned, we all sinned.

David, king of Israel and a poet, asks God in Psalm 51:1–4 to forgive him for having an affair with another man's wife and then setting her husband up to be killed. Unlike Adam in Genesis 3, David took full responsibility for his actions, even saying that sin was inside of him ever since he was conceived in his mother's womb (v. 5). This *hits us off* with the truth that, like David, you and I were sinful since we were conceived in our mother's womb because it was passed on to us by our father Adam.

In summary, Adam and Eve broke God's law and were cut off from their supply of life, both physically and spiritually. In response, they felt shame as they realized they were naked and no longer pure, and this reality caused them to go on the run from God. The Bible tells us that when sin entered into the world through Adam, so did death, and both have been passed down to each and every one of us because of Adam, who is our father and represented us.

How can man and woman be restored to God when such sin separates us? The answer is found in the next chapter.

A GOSPEL Rap

"SIN INTRODUCED"

Verse 1:

Yea, He started when his cousin told him, "Hold this."
Pass it to the fiend walkin' by who need a dope fix.
Passed him a stack of Jacksons, 8 ball baggys, no tens.
Take it to the trap house on the Ave with the broke fence.

Fast-forward, lights camera, action with a slow lens.
No hands Wakka Flakka, clockin' dollas, no sense (cents).
Freeway-interstate push and pullin' on those bricks.
"Do you wanna ride," Do or Die Po Pimp, on Chrome Rims.

Got a call from his brothers, not the Jonas,
Got connected with Colombians who'll leave that throat slit.
Got him tipsy, gone off Patron sips & coke sniffs.
Promised to, spot him if he push the bottom weight . . . Gold's
    Gym.

Told him, the long arm of the law swings, don't flinch.
And if they get his dope pinched (shh, shh, shh), don't snitch
As long as he stayed loyal, these boys'll always be close friends,
Money laundered thru the cycle & recycle, no rinse.

Hook: See how quick the game will flip it on ya.
All ya boys snitchin' on ya, 5.0 inchin' on ya.

Verse 2:

Now the homie connected, his game's the truth, no fibs.

Life is C.R.E.A.M. filled, Cuz; that cake call it Hostess.

Extravagant his home is, kinda like the show cribs

Livin' on unlimited supply, stay High like Voltage.

Flying nothing but that First Class, call Him Postage.

Roguish, Baltimore (Raven) Ravin', dancing with glow sticks

Bi-Coastal movin' both ends, Hyphy out in Oakland.

Movin dro, that blow, coke or snow and ya know Thizz

His bro's pinched, like a roach clip when He phoned him

To set up deal wit some country boys, no Oakridge.

He got roped in, trusting one of his old friends;

Briefcases open, DEA closed in.

Showin' no emotion, his own kin was the culprit.

Leavin' son set up and pinched just like a clothespin.

He gave up his connection, now they gonna have to fold him.

You prolly saw him on the news, face down floatin'.

Verse 3:

I gotta switch it up, to the rhyme scheme listen up,

This whole song is dedicated to the sin in us.

Dude got smashed all because He snitched it up;

Broke the 4th & 9th crack commandments, remember Biggie
     Cuz?

Breakin' commandments, that's called sinning, Cuz.
And thanks to Adam, that's how sin entered us.
Genesis 3, is where we gotta pick it up:
Adam broke God's commands, and Adam represented us.

We were once connected to God, open friend to us.
Thru our father Adam, yea, everybody kin to us.
Chapter 11 verse 44 in Leviticus.
God's Holy, so homie that one sin distanced us.

Now we're prisoners, to death God sentenced us
Because the wages of sin is death like a pension, Cuz.
Every day we walk the yard with sin pimpin' us
Got that penalty and price is on our head like *fitted* Cuz.

5

P—Penalty and Price

As we continue reading Genesis 3, verse 21 puts us up on game about the penalty for sin, which is death. If we read over this verse too fast, we'll miss the *bangin'* point of this Scripture. In the last chapter, we saw the proof that sin entered the world when Adam and Eve ran from God to hide their shame and nakedness. The proof that death entered the world is seen when God clothed Adam and Eve with threads made of animal skin.

Since death was the penalty for sin, God had every right to smash Adam and Eve, but He chose to smash an animal in their place as a substitution. That animal paid the price for the man and woman who had transgressed God's command.

This substitution is kind of like a stunt double in a movie. When we go to the movies to watch an action flick, we'll *peep* scenes laced with explosives, and often out of these explosions walks the main character without a scratch. The reason the actor seems unharmed is because a stunt double, someone with professional training in dealing with explosives, who looks like the main actor, is hired to take the place of the main actor and perform these stunts.

Acting is Hollywood. Sin is real life. Because the penalty for sin is death, God chose to let Adam and Eve live and smashed the animal in their place, and He used the skin of the animal to cover up their guilt and shame from the sin they committed.

So at this point, sin and death have entered the world. At the same time, as a result of God's loving-kindness toward His creation, grace and mercy enter as well. Grace means being given something you didn't earn or work for, and mercy is when someone shows you compassion rather than anger. God allowed Adam and Eve to live physically even though they deserved to die, and, rather than take His anger out on them, He gave them clothes to cover up their shame.

We've all heard the rhyme, "If you do the crime, you do the time," but in the hood we know this is not always true. The code of the streets calls for a ***no-snitchin' rule***, meaning if you get pinched or witness a crime, when police question you, you offer no answers that will lead to arrest of the criminal. If the person pinched ***takes the rap*** for the crime and the real criminal remains free, street credibility is earned for the person who took the rap and did the time for the crime. They pay the price for someone else's crime.

So peeps in the hood are used to the idea of someone stepping in and taking the punishment for something they didn't do; they can relate this concept to the price for sin, so don't think for a minute they can't understand this idea of substitutionary atonement for sin. The price for breaking the law on the streets can be jail, probation, or even a bid in prison; it all depends on the seriousness of the crime. When we discuss the price for sin—breaking God's righteous law—we have to **step up our game** when it comes to understanding what God requires.

God told the people of Israel, "For the life of the flesh is in the blood, and I have given it to you upon the altar to make atonement for your souls; for it is the blood that makes atonement for the soul" (Leviticus 17:11). The word **atonement** in the Bible means to cover something up, and God said the only way sin could be covered up was by the shedding of blood. Now earlier in Leviticus, in chapters 1–7, God instructs His people on the types of sacrifices that were to be offered: animals without blemish or stain. A worthy, perfect sacrifice, represented in a valued possession of the sinner, was necessary to pay the price of one's sins. Hebrews 9:22 explains: "And according to the law almost all things are purified with blood, and without shedding of blood there is no remission." The word **remission** means forgiveness, and God is saying that He cannot forgive the sins of men and women unless something is put to death by the shedding of its blood. This is the only way sinners can continue to live and have their sins covered.

Unlike the people of Israel who owned and sacrificed animals, neither you nor I are sacrificing animals to God for our sins. So we have to ask the question, *How are my sins being atoned or covered?* The Bible tells us that God gives us two payment plans when it comes to our sins. The first option is we can pay for our own sins after we die by spending all of eternity in a place of torment called hell. Since we defined death earlier as separation from God, Romans 6:23 tells us that the "wages of sin is death." This means that when a sinner chooses this option, he is essentially telling God, "I don't want to pay for my sins now, so I'm gonna wait until later and store up my debt until the day I have to face judgment." It's kind of like what we saw happen to Lil Wayne and T.I. They were arrested for breaking the law, posted bail, were released, went to trial, were found guilty, and then were given a certain day they had to report to prison.

Like Lil Wayne and T.I., you and I have to face judgment. Hebrews 9:27 tells us that every single one of us will die one day, and after we die, we will face *the* judgment. When we are judged by God—if we chose option one—He will find us guilty because we chose to pay for our sins on our own, and we will spend all of eternity being tormented and separated from a right relationship with God. This payment plan has no ending. It's not a three-to-nine- or a two-to-four-year bid with an option for good behavior—it never ends!

So what other option for sinners is there? God has provided a far superior option, and in the next chapter we'll learn about this much better option for payment of our sins.

A GOSPEL Rap

"PENALTY & PRICE"

Hook: You already know (already know, already know)
There's a penalty and price for the sin in ya life—aayyyyyyy.

Verse 1:
Imagine livin' in debt, never getting ahead
Like ya budget's Piru, infinite Red.
Creditors harassing, wishin ya dead
Police kick in the do', wave the .44 'bout an inch from ya head.

Cuffed to the bed, stuck in the chest, one to the head
Thought ya was above the law, now ya under arrest.
Extradited from ya crib to a holdin' cell
Judge put ya debt on display for all to see—"show n tell."

Put you in a debtors' prison, all ya cheddar's missin,
You got no way to pay 'em back, AYO . . . better listen.
For ya crime the Judge gotta give ya proper recognition:
Capital Punishment, death penalty by definition.

Whooooaa . . . real talk, ya really guilty.
Never was so Fresh and Clean, but really filthy.
Whooaa . . . now whatcha know about that?
Nothing, ya was hustlin' for the money from a paper brown bag.

Verse 2:

I was born in a world where it's tough to live (tough to live),

For all of us raised in the hood, we must admit (must admit).

Our environment had pressure, we was under it (under it).

Bein' poor had momma seeking income that'll supplement.

All alone, TV showed us "Fame" we lovin in it,

Flicks showed us sex, we lust for it, can't get enough of it.

Older dudes discipled us on how to pick up a chick

We could pull 'em if push weight to flex, muscle men.

Every day we see the custom rims/started hustlin'

Wanna be trap stars, hold heat—no oven mitt . . .

This is sin, like BET's the game, it just suck us in.

Leaves ya fellowship wit God broke like some bummin' men.

The world's our debtors' prison, flesh the jumpsuit, custom fit,

Sin gotta penalty and price, (what is it) shed blood it is.

Verse 3:

You already know the price, (am I guilty) sho' ya right!

Leviticus 17:11 the atonement plight.

Atonement means to cover up, like plastic on a sofa, right?

If there's a stain ya'd prolly see the dot wit no polka, right? (right)

Yoo . . . move wit me like an ocean tide,

God demands blood for our atonement, that's no surprise.

Remember Adam sinned (yea), this'll blow ya mind,

An animal substituted for Adam's which made for his

   atonement right

Yoo . . . Seriously Adam lived, jokes aside.

Even tho the wage of sin is death, no mo' life.

Connect the dots, I guarantee this'll blow ya high,

This is how you live thru every 3rd shift, overnight.

Cuz of sin God shoulda crushed ya like soda ice,

But He let's ya live because He toll'd the Christ.

His atonement for sin foreclosed its price,

Let the Gospel shine on ya walk, motion light.

6

E—Enter Jesus

At this point in the story, the scene is dark. Sin and death are all around us, and we need a better option to pay for our sins. At last, the story gets infinitely and eternally better when Jesus Christ enters the scene! John 1:1 tells us that Jesus has always been God— He is not a created being—and He is equal with God the Father and God the Holy Spirit. Jesus, being fully God, decided to leave heaven and come to earth for one reason: to become our second option for payment of our sins.

Jesus put on human flesh, the apostle John writes in his Gospel (1:14) and came to live here on earth. Think about it—we don't have a God who is so *bougie* that He stayed distant from us, rather He came to the *gulliness* of our world and lived in the filth. Yet Jesus never became dirty because He is God, and God cannot sin!

Here is where we have to ask ourselves: *Why would Jesus leave heaven to come here when we're all trying to get up out of this "hell on earth" to get to heaven? Ain't that backward?* Jesus answers our question when He declares, "The

Son of Man did not come to be served, but to serve, and to give His life a ransom for many" (Matthew 20:28). Real talk: This passage tells us that Jesus came to earth to step in and pay the penalty and price for our sin that neither you nor I could pay! The word *for* in this passage means to be put in the place of someone else. That someone was us, sinful humans!

The word *"**ransom**"* spoken by Jesus was often used when someone would buy a slave out of slavery. Since slavery in America has been abolished for 150 years, what does this have to do with you and me? The Scriptures connect our sins to slavery. Jesus said whoever commits a sin is a slave to sin (John 8:34), and Paul the apostle says the same thing in Romans 6:15–23. Because you and I have been sinful ever since we were in our mother's womb, and because no one had to teach us how to sin (we practice it every day), it's safe to say that you and I were born and have lived enslaved to sin!

See how bangin' Jesus is? He came to step into our place to pay our sin debt, and He also bought us out of our slavery to sin!

All four Gospels give us eyewitness accounts of Jesus' death on a cross: Matthew 27:35–50; Mark 15:23–37; Luke 23:33–46; and John 19:18–30. Now when we read these passages in Scripture, we will see that each eyewitness account is a little different, as some accounts have details others don't. This does not mean that any or all of these accounts aren't true; it just means we're reading what different people saw when they watched Jesus die. The same type of story took place a few years ago when ***Tookie Williams*** was executed by lethal injection. I read at least four different reporters' news articles that reported what they saw when they were there when Tookie was executed, and each report had differences in Tookie's comments and the way the needle was injected into his vein. All four agreed on the main details; they were all there to witness Tookie's execution, they watched him die, and they reported what they saw. We must keep this in mind when we read the true accounts of Jesus' death in Scripture.

Most importantly, God commanded that every sacrifice offered for sins had to be without blemish or stain, remember? Hebrews 7:26 and 9:22–26 tell us that Jesus never committed a single sin during His thirty-three-plus years of life on earth, which means He has always been, and still is, and will always be without blemish or stain! One might be asking, "How can we be sure that Jesus' sacrifice qualifies for the payment of my sin?"

That's a good question that Romans 4:24–25 answers by ***puttin' us up on game*** to the truth. When Jesus rose from the grave three days after His death (Matthew 28), His resurrection was living proof that God was satisfied with Jesus' offering Himself in our place, as our substitution, and we could now be ***justified***. The word *justified* means to be legally declared not guilty!

So now, because we have Jesus' one-time sacrifice, you and I don't need the blood of any animal to atone for our sins. Jesus didn't just pay for our sins; He also washed them away! Forty days after He resurrected, Jesus ascended back to heaven because His mission was complete. Acts 1:9–11 promises us that Jesus will return one day to let those of us who chose the second option for the payment of our sins to enter into a never-ending, face-to-face fellowship with God!

A GOSPEL Rap

"ENTER JESUS"

Hook: Enter Jesus, Enter Jesus, Enter Jesus, into a world of sin
(Come, come wit it, come wit it, Savior—come, come wit it,
        come wit it save us)

Verse 1:
Real talk, here we are, the scene is dark
All of humanity's ruled by a population of deceitful hearts.
Jeremiah 13:23, evil hearts
Can't change the fact they rockin' spots like Measles Scars.

Distorted, supported by the world's rhythm like lead guitars
We seek the crowd's approval cuz we need applause.
God given commands we ignore and breach His laws
Guilty, we need a substitute like when a teacher's off.

Introducing the God man, Christ Jesus, Ya'll
Volunteered to rescue us when we are flawed.
Eternally equal with God the Father, He is God.
Eternally equal with the Holy Spirit, He is God.

Hebrews 7:26, sinless, He is God.
Mark 2:7, forgiveness, He is God.
Luke 2:49, 'bout the Father's business, He is God.
I said six times that He is God, because we are not.

Verse 2:
The penalty for sin's on our head like a **skully** is.
He wasn't too bougie to stay away from our **gulliness**.
The beautiful Savior lovingly embraced our ugliness
To lead us Wildcats to the crown like Tubby Smith.

Isaiah 53:2, He wasn't handsome or pretty;
Came to give His life as a ransom for many.
Ransom means to buy a slave outta slavery;
John 8:34 sin alone's what's enslaving me.

Romans 6:15 to the chapter's end
We obey sin our master therefore can never master it.
Romans 6:23, our reward hazardous,
So Jesus stepped in to absorb God's wrath for sin.

While we were dead, Jesus gave His life for sin,
Enduring, our scourging and torture with no Vicodin.
To God it made sense (like what son), like a dime is ten;
So He could Rise from the Underworld like Lykins did.

Verse 3:

John 14:6, no one else is qualified

To lead wayward sinners back to the Father's side.

Muhammad, Buddha, Krishna—all them died.

Psalm 51:5, they was born in sin; disqualified.

Now here's a truth more hypnotic than rims customized:

Jesus' resurrection proves we can be justified.

Justified mean to be declared free

From the penalty and price for the sin that ensnares me.

It's hard to swallow, chew on this like Carefree:

This could be ya first day of Christmas, no partridge in a pear tree.

The Spotless lamb is Abraham's ram, no Aries;

All who accept Him live in Jubilee without the Cherries.

Trust me son, He alone is that dude.

Peep Chapter 28 verse 20 of Matthew.

He never leaves those he saves, let me ask you

Has he entered ya heart and saved ya from the wrath due?

7

L—Life Everlasting

J ust as our story began with man having life because he was connected to God, the supplier of life, our story ends the same way. Jesus said in John 14:6, "I am the way, the truth and the life. No one comes to the Father except through Me." This statement brings us to a major fork in the road. We can say Jesus is no one of significance. We can say Jesus is one of many ways to the Father. Or we can say Jesus is the only way to the Father.

We live in a day where people tell us that we can have our own relationship with God on our terms and we don't need Jesus. Others tell us that Jesus was a good man who never claimed to be God and we should only follow His *example* to find God ourselves. Still others tell us Jesus is less than God and we can find God through other men who are like Jesus, such as Muhammad, Buddha, Hare Krishna, or even our favorite celebrities.

I don't know about you, but I don't like it when others put words in my mouth. As we look at the Bible, it's clear to see that Jesus never said a lot of the things other people may tell us. He told us from His own mouth that He is *the* way, *the* truth, and *the* life. Jesus is the only qualified middleman to put us back in connection with God who is the supplier of life! Today He still says He is the only way to God.

Life everlasting is what is promised to those who choose Jesus' payment option for their sin. Jesus says that the one requirement for receiving life everlasting is believing that His life and resurrection are enough to pay for our sins (John 11:25–26). If this is true, there is no hope for having life everlasting outside of Jesus Christ. (Even the men I mentioned earlier needed to turn to Jesus and believe that what He did was good enough to get them off the hook from eternal punishment, and if they didn't, they do not have access to God or life everlasting.) The Bible tells us that if we believe Jesus' work was good enough to pay for our sin, we will be saved! (For example, see John 3:16–18; 5:24–25; 6:40; 1 Peter 2:24–25.)

In America, it is one of our rights to not suffer double jeopardy; meaning, if we are found innocent of a crime once, we cannot be tried again for it. Another truth that applies here is the plea bargain. Often if someone is pinched and they are guilty of a crime, they will admit they are guilty to avoid going to trial so they can receive a lesser sentence than if they go to trial and are found guilty. This is also true when it comes to God. If we confess that we are guilty and deserve to pay for our own sins, but accept Jesus' perfect life, death, and resurrection in our place, we essentially take the plea bargain that not only saves us from paying for our sin but also does away with our old rap sheet. In return, God gives us Jesus' spotless record! Real talk: Why would anyone turn down a deal like that, especially when you look at the eternal benefit of living face-to-face with God!

First Corinthians 15:12–58 promises all of us who take the plea bargain that, one day, we will be with our Lord in His crib called heaven and never become sick or die again! Even better than this, in heaven we will never struggle with sin anymore and will never break any of God's laws ever again! Most importantly, we will never have to be separated from God ever again. We will be in open fellowship with, and eternally connected to, the supplier of life!

A GOSPEL Rap

"LIFE EVERLASTING"

Hook: It don't stop (naw) and it won't stop (naw)

Verse 1

Come, come, witcha boy, let's celebrate with ya, boy
How a holy God saved sinners from a hellish fate.
Eternal life starts way before we cross the **cellophane**.
Oh, you didn't know, ayo . . . let me tell it straight.

I was born an enemy of the whole Trinity,
Not because of race but because of the sin in me.
Every day my heart beat for sin like a Tympani
In harmony with the world's system like Symphony.

Fam, I ain't blowing bricks and smoking like a Chimney;
I used to be under a curse like the Kennedys.
Until God the Son gave me an epiphany
That turns boys to men while on bended knees.

You shoulda smashed me, You shoulda bashed me;
But instead Ya gave me life everlasting.
You shoulda murdered me, but became a curse for me;
Set up me with never ending life for eternity.

Verse 2

Come, come with ya, boy, let's celebrate
How a holy God saved sinners from a hellish fate.
Eternal life starts way before we cross the cellophane
Oh, you didn't know, ayo . . . let me tell it straight.

Eternal life starts the minute Christ saves us,
2 Cor 5:17, He remakes us.
The old us is dead, the new us remains, cuz
Romans 8:9 the Spirit of God invades us.

Real talk He sanctifies and sustains us,
Even tho we live in flesh that incarnates us.
And He's gonna finish the work to reshape us.
When we die we'll be with God face-to-face, Cuz.

You shoulda smashed me, You shoulda bashed me;
But instead Ya gave me life everlasting.
You shoulda murdered me, but became a curse for me;
Set up me with never ending life for eternity.

Verse 3

Come, come with ya, boy, let's celebrate
How a holy God saved sinners from a hellish fate
Eternal life starts way before we cross the cellophane
Oh you didn't know, ayo . . . let me tell it straight.

Let me put you up on that zoe (zoe)
Up close looks fuzzy, fall back, it's a Monet.
Let me make it clear as a goose that's so gray
Saints alone can viva la vida, like Cold Play.

We will never feel the heat, not a fever that's low grade,
In Heaven we will never fall into sin, no way . . .
In Heaven we always be wit God, we won't stray;
In Heaven our walk and fellowshippin' is hittin' wit no K's.

You shoulda smashed me, You shoulda bashed me;
But instead Ya gave me life everlasting.
You shoulda murdered me, but became a curse for me;
Set up me with never ending life for eternity.

What Now?

The first seven chapters walked you through the GOSPEL. You have been presented truth as an urban dweller that you may be hearing for the first time; or, as the suburban dweller, truth you have heard in the urban context in a way that can help you communicate with those seeking Him in our cities across America. God hit me off with this same truth when I was about to turn sixteen years old.

As a child I was baptized into the Roman Catholic Church and from the age of five went to church on a regular basis, but neither baptism nor church attendance paid for my sins. By the time I was thirteen, I was running the streets and had been committing crimes from theft to vandalism since I was nine! I heard the sermons, I went with my church to reach out to kids who lived in the projects, but I was still on my way to pay for my own sins because I didn't accept the plea bargain that Jesus was offering me. At just the right time, while I was contemplating leaving the nickel-and-dime bags of weed I was selling to move on to pushin' more weight, all the while facing issues with the police—God saved me.

On March 31, 1996, a pastor, George W. Westlake Jr., shared the Gospel with me at church on a Sunday night, and I took the plea bargain. I have been alive ever since!

I would be robbing you of life everlasting if I didn't ask you to think through these questions:

1. Read Romans 3:23 and answer this question: *Are you willing to admit, like Adam, that you have broken God's laws by sinning?*
2. Read Psalm 51:5 and Romans 6:23 and answer this question: *Are you willing to admit you have been a sinner since before you were born and every day afterwards and that you deserve to die?*
3. Read Romans 5:12 and Hebrews 9:27 and answer this question: *Are you willing to admit that you will have to face death because you are a sinner?*
4. Read Hebrews 7:26 and 1 Peter 2:24 and answer this question: *Do you believe that Jesus Christ, who has always been God, clothed Himself in human flesh so that He alone could live a life that would never break a single one of God's laws so He could die by shedding His blood in your place to pay the penalty and price for your sin?*
5. Read John 14:6 and answer this question: *Are you willing to admit that Jesus is the only person qualified to pay for your sins?*
6. Read Matthew 28 and Romans 4:24–25 and answer

this question: *Do you believe that Jesus resurrected from the grave three days after His death, and that His resurrection proves the sacrifice He made in our place pleased God, and by His blood alone we can have forgiveness of our sins?*

If you answered yes to all of the above questions, I invite you to read this statement of confession to God as you ask to take the plea bargain. Say it from your heart, as a prayer to God your Creator:

God, real talk: I know I am a sinner. I see in the Bible where it only takes one sin to lose connection to You, and during my whole life I've committed way more than one sin. I admit that I am guilty. I admit that I deserve to die, but I just got put up on game that You have offered me a way to admit my guilt, and not have to pay for my sins, by accepting the fact that Jesus paid my penalty and my price for my sin, even though He was never guilty of breaking any of Your laws. I believe Jesus rose from the grave three days later to prove His death was good enough to pay for my debt. Today, God, I ask for Your plea bargain that is only found in the work that Jesus did. I ask You to free me from my slavery to sin and become my new master. I've never walked with You before, so I ask You to bring other people into my life who have taken Your plea bargain, and have them help me understand my new life and how to adjust to life outside of the prison of sin. Thank You for saving me from being eternally cut off from life! In Jesus' name I pray, Amen.

Now I've got to **keep it 100** with you. Just reading over this prayer does not automatically mean you've been set free from sin. You will still have struggles with sin; the sin nature is still in you. But there will no longer be a desire to live a life controlled by sin. The Bible teaches that if you prayed this prayer and were saved by grace through faith, there will be evidence of change that will take place in your life, such as:

1. For the first time, you will have the desire to glorify God by saying no to sin because of God the Holy Spirit living inside you (Romans 8:9–13).

2. For the first time, you will truly love God and daily begin to fall "out of love" with the world (1 John 2:15–17).

3. For the first time, you will truly desire to know God more by reading His Word, the Bible, and praying to Him (1 Peter 2:1–3 and 1 Thessalonians 5:17).

4. For the first time, you will truly realize that we struggle with sin every day, and we will ask God to forgive us (1 John 1:8–10).

5. For the first time, you will want to stop committing the sins we used to love, and show God our love for Him is real by repenting (2 Corinthians 7:9–11).

6. For the first time, you will want to be around other people who have a real relationship with Jesus like we do, because we truly love them (1 John 4:7–8).

7. For the first time, you now desire to be part of

a community (or church) of other Christians we can live with, confess our sins to, and worship the Lord with (Hebrews 10:24–25).

8. For the first time, you will desire to share the Gospel with people who do not know about Jesus or His plea bargain (Matthew 28:19–20).

This list is made up of changes that you should begin to see in your life as time goes on. The best decision you can make after you prayed the above prayer is to get plugged into a local church that is healthy. Before we move on to how to get plugged into a local church, let's unpack the terms *local church* and *healthy*.

Let's realize that the local church is not identified by a building that people gather in but rather by the people themselves who have this in common: They've all taken the plea bargain offered to them by Jesus Christ. There are Christians worldwide who are not allowed to gather publicly to worship God, yet they are as much a part of the **body of Christ** as other Christians who gather in a designated church building on Sunday. So when we speak of the local church, we're talking about the people of God who have asked Christ to save them from the penalty of their sins. Biblically we see the church called the body of Christ in 1 Corinthians 12:27 and Ephesians 4:12.

To locate a healthy church, examine what I call the three Ps: the preaching, the people, and the process.

The Preaching. Healthy preaching shows itself when

the preacher clearly communicates what the Bible says in such a way that the listener has an understanding of the passage and is able to apply this passage to their everyday life. Healthy preaching contains a Gospel-centered message. This means the preacher's sermon contains the GOSPEL as explained in chapters 2–7. He allows listeners to wrestle with the reality of their own personal sin and need for a Savior. He identifies Jesus Christ as being the only qualified Savior to save sinners from the penalty and price of their sin.

Healthy preaching also teaches the listener good theology that is grounded in what the Bible says. Good theology equips Christians with knowledge of who God is, what He does and does not do, and how we are to live for Him daily. Earlier we defined theology as studying God. With this in mind, a healthy local church creates an atmosphere for Christians to joyfully spend their time studying the God who saved them. A healthy church will have healthy preaching.

The People. In every local church you will find two groups of people: leaders and lay members (or nonleaders). The Bible identifies two types of leaders in the local church: elders and deacons. The qualifications of these leaders are found in 1 Timothy 3:1–13 and Titus 1:6–16. A healthy church will have leaders who meet the qualifications seen in Scripture. Never be ashamed to ask leaders in a church that you are considering plugging into if their leaders meet the biblical qualifications.

A way to measure the health of the lay members in the church is by looking at their commitment to the local church. Commitment to a local church can be demonstrated in many ways, including members regularly attending gatherings in addition to Sunday service, using their *spiritual gifts* to encourage those in our church, finding ways to help with projects, and by supporting the church through financial giving that is predetermined, regular, sacrificial, and cheerful. A healthy church will have healthy leaders and lay members.

The Process. Every Christian, no matter whether he or she is a leader or a lay member in a local church, has been given the same job description simply known as the Great Commission. Jesus Himself gave the Great Commission in Matthew 28:19–20, declaring, "Go therefore and make disciples of all nations, baptizing them in the name of the Father and of the Son and of the Holy Spirit, teaching them to observe all things that I have commanded you; and lo, I am with you always, even to the end of the age." If every Christian is a part of the body of Christ, and if the body of Christ has corporately been given one job description, the process of every local church should be to preach the Gospel, lead sinners to Christ, take them by the hand and live life with them while teaching about the God who saved them—so they may be sent out to preach the Gospel and start this process over again. A healthy church will practice this healthy process.

A couple of good books that go into more detail

about what a healthy church looks like are *Nine Marks of a Healthy Church* and *What Is a Healthy Church?*, both by Pastor Mark Dever.

Now I'd like to suggest a few practical ways on how you can get plugged into a healthy local church. Real talk: You can't find a healthy church unless you look for one. You can start with the Internet to learn some of the basics. Look up local churches in your area and then through a search engine (Goggle or Yahoo, for example) go to their websites to look at any information about their preaching, people, and process. (Most websites will have little if anything on the people; to learn about the people, you will need to visit the church.) You also can talk with trusted friends you know and ask them about the church they attend. In addition, you can look up churches in your local phone book and begin to call them to collect information about their church. After you have identified a few churches that interest you, take the following three steps.

Step One: Find out what they believe. You can do this by asking them for their statement of faith. (It may be on their website.) A statement of faith is the document that informs people what the church believes and teaches. The essential teachings of Christianity should be present in the statement of faith of a healthy church—such essentials as the Bible is without error or contradiction and is the standard of what we believe and how we behave; God is not a created being and has always existed as Father, Son, and Holy Spirit at the same time; man was created in the im-

age of God but willingly fell into sin, which means he dis-
obeyed God and cannot be brought back into fellowship
with God without being saved by a Savior. A local church,
as part of the body of Christ, should also believe Jesus is
the true Savior for sinners; and through Jesus Christ alone
we are saved by grace through faith.

The statement of faith should also address the fact
that the Holy Spirit lives in every Christian and provides
us with the ability to say no to sin and yes to holy living,
showing that we have been born again. In addition, those
in a healthy church should believe Jesus' promise that He
will return again, physically and visibly to rule with us.
(Acts 1:11). A good book that walks you through the essentials of the faith is *Systematic Theology: An Introduction
to Biblical Doctrine* by Wayne Grudem. I recommend you
read it.

Step Two: Visit the church(es) you are interested in.
Then set a time to meet with the pastor or other leader.
Many pastors and leaders find joy in taking time to get to
know their visitors and potential future members. I suggest that during this meeting, if time allows, ask the pastor or leader questions about their statement of faith, how
they are active in fulfilling the Great Commission, and
other issues or concerns that you find important. If time
does not allow, find out how you can schedule a follow-up
meeting with the pastor or leader to discuss such issues.
During your meeting it would be wise to ask what the
process looks like for someone to become a member of the

local church and how members can serve in ministry.

Take time to examine the preaching, people, and process of the church before you consider joining. The challenge is not to rush membership but at the same time not to drag your feet either. Many Christians today fall victim to church hopping, meaning they go to one church for a while, fail to land and plug in and then start going to another church abruptly only to repeat this process later. We were not saved to just attend a church service but rather lock in and serve with our brothers and sisters in the body of Christ. A good book that addresses the beauty of church membership is *Stop Dating the Church* by Joshua Harris.

Step Three: Pray. Ask the Lord to provide you with peace on which church He desires you to become a member of and then contact the church and find out how you can join and begin to serve. First Corinthians 12:11 tells us that God the Holy Spirit has given each individual believer a spiritual gift that is to be used not for our own glory or reputation but rather for the encouragement of all the other believers in our local church. Many Christians today are using their talents to preach the Gospel to sinners but fail in using their spiritual gift in their local church. Both saints and sinners have been given talents by God, yet only saints have been given spiritual gifts by God the Holy Spirit. One way to examine your use of spiritual gifts and talents is to ask yourself, *Are nonbelievers doing what I'm doing in their everyday life?* to help identify your talents, and then follow up with this question, *How can*

I do what non-believers cannot do in the local church? to help identify your spiritual gift. A good book that identifies ways you can contribute to the local church is *What Is a Healthy Church Member?* by Thabiti M. Anyabwile.

Being a part of a healthy local church will provide you with the strength and encouragement that you need to preach the GOSPEL in the hood for years to come so that you can follow up with them after the concert, sermon, and outreach ends. The natural follow-up to preaching the GOSPEL is leading people into healthy churches. One great challenge in urban ministry is the fact that there are many churches yet very few of them are healthy.

Our nations are in desperate need of more healthy churches that have healthy pulpits, people, and a healthy process located in the urban community. Healthy churches will not become common in the urban context until the Gospel is preached; so let's get out there and preach the GOSPEL:

> the **G**ood news of God's image,
> **O**pen fellowship,
> **S**in introduced,
> the **P**enalty and Price,
> **E**nter Jesus, and
> **L**ife everlasting.

THEBONICAL GLOSSARY

Atonement—Blood from a sacrifice that is used to cover up the sin of a sinner so he may continue to live. *When Jesus died on the cross, His blood was shed, and it not only atoned for my sins, it washed them away!*

Baby mama/Baby daddy—A man and woman who are not married to each yet have a child together and remain unmarried after the child is born. *A ministry of our church should be one that provides biblical counsel on relationships so that baby mamas and baby daddys can become biblical husbands and wives.*

Baby mama/Baby daddy drama—When another man or woman comes into the relational picture of the baby mama or baby daddy, jealousy and hurt feelings are expressed in such a way that it leads to stressful and hostile situations. *Let's pray that the Lord removes the bitterness from her baby daddy's heart so there will be no more baby mama and baby daddy drama between them.*

Bangin'—Something that is appealing or pleasing. *The Gospel is a bangin' message.*

Body of Christ—The body of Christ is all people who have accepted the plea bargain offered to them by Jesus Christ. The body of Christ is another name for the church. The church refers to those who believe in Jesus as their Savior; it is not primarily about the building where they meet to worship. *I thank the Lord for saving me and making me a part of the body of Christ.*

Bougie—Something that is expensive or someone who thinks they are better than others. *Yo, since shorty moved out of the hood and into the suburbs, she got all bougie.*

Cartel—A unit or corporation of businesses that used to compete against each other; often used to describe drug lords who combine to make one new business. *The Juarez Cartel is known to have connections in Kansas City.*

Cellophane—Short for "cellophane tape." Metaphorically used in the Gospel rap song "Life Everlasting," to speak of the Christian finishing their race by crossing the finish line and breaking the tape. *"Eternal life starts way before we cross the cellophane"* means eternal life for the Christian starts before they get to heaven.

Chop it up—To converse with someone in-depth on a particular subject. *Ayo, let's chop it up about the Gospel.*

Cuz—A term of endearment; short for "cousin." The word is used often when speaking to someone you are in fellowship with, not always used when describing a blood relative. *What's good, cuz, you wanna go to church with me?*

Death—Being separated from God. *The Bible says those who reject the plea bargain God offers through Jesus Christ will die a second death.*

Don't hate—To criticize someone or something based on appearance, reputation, or their renderings. *Don't hate cuz I'm on the block preachin' the Gospel!*

Fellowship—A word that describes a person's relationship with someone they have something in common with. *Ricky got jumped into the Crips last night; he's in fellowship with them now.*

Fitted—A baseball-style cap that is one size that is not adjustable (i.e., 7 3/8). *Ayo fam, I'm gonna rock my KC fitted today to rep my city.*

Gulliness—An adjective derived from the root word "gully," which means unpolished, raw, grimy, or real; the opposite of bougie. *Yo, real talk, Jesus came to the gulliness of this world to deal with the real of our sin.*

Hit off—The act of presenting new information to someone. Normally this phrase places a noun or pronoun between the words hit and off to identify the person who received the information. *The Lord used me to hit them off with the Gospel the other night.*

Hood—The city neighborhood; lifestyle choices that affirm one is from the *hood*. *I know I live in sin; I'm so hood, though.*

Kevin Hart—An African-American comedian known to urban listeners for his clever humor.

Keep it 100—Not withholding truth, to keep it real. *I gotta keep it 100; we were all born in sin.*

I see you—A term of recognition when someone wears, says, or does something that is impressive. *Okay, you just told me the Gospel. I see you.*

Justified—Being declared not guilty for our sins by God because our sinful rap sheet was replaced by Jesus' perfect life. *When I took the plea bargain God offers through Jesus Christ, I was justified,* or declared not guilty.

Movin' weight—Selling a large quantity of illegal drugs. *Before the Lord saved me, I used to move weight like crazy yo.*

No-snitchin' rule—An unofficial, yet respected, understanding in the inner city that says witnesses of a crime are not to spill to police what they saw. If they do, repercussions will be distributed. *They pinched Lucky and he snitched, let's get him when he gets out.*

Peep—To pay attention to what someone says or does. *Yo, peep what I'm 'bout to say!*

Pinched—To get caught committing a crime or to be placed under arrest. *They pinched my boy last night, man.*

Put up on game—Present new information to someone about something they had no real knowledge or understanding of before. *I just got put up on game about the Gospel.*

Ransom—A word used to buy back slaves. *Jesus came to earth to be the ransom that bought me out of my slavery to sin.*

Real talk—Saying something of absolute truth, synonymous with **Keep it 100**. *A biblical parallel for real talk is when Jesus said, "verily, verily."*

Regeneration—An event that takes place when the Gospel is preached to a sinner, and God the Holy

Spirit gives life everlasting to the sinner because they believe in the work Jesus did to pay for their sins. *Real talk, I used to live foul before I heard the Gospel, which led to God the Holy Spirit regeneratin' me, meaning He saved me.*

Remission—A word used to describe the forgiveness of sin. *The blood of Jesus had to be shed for me to have forgiveness for my sins, because God said there is no remission for sin if blood is not shed* (see Hebrews 9:22).

Replica—An exact copy of something. *Yo, I got that replica jersey, son!*

Rock/rockin'—The act of wearing something; figuratively used to describe emotions as well. *My dude rockin' them new Jordans is rockin' a big smile on his face too!*

Saved—A word used to describe those who took the plea bargain God offers through Jesus. *I was born in sin, but was saved when I believed in the work Jesus did to pay off my sin debt.*

Skully—Short for "skull cap," which is a hat that is worn that has no brim; normally worn when temperatures are cool. *Ayo, its cold outside, I'm gonna rock this skully instead of my fitted.*

Smugglin'—The act of transporting illegal drugs from one area to another. *Before I got saved, I was smugglin' weed, yo!*

Spillin'—To voice one's knowledge or opinion on a topic, synonymous with ***chop it up***. *Yea, that pastor was spillin' the Gospel on the block!*

Spiritual gift—A Holy Spirit–given ability that is used to encourage other Christians. These gifts are listed in Romans 12:6–8; 1 Corinthians 12:8–10, 28–30; Ephesians 4:11; and 1 Peter 4:10–11. *Real talk: 1 Corinthians 12:11 tells us that every believer has been given at least one spiritual gift by God the Holy Spirit.*

Step up your game—Seeking to upgrade or improve one's presentation or knowledge. *If you wanna rap for Jesus, you need to step up your game in the Scriptures.*

Swag—The way a person projects his attitude, or the way one lives and/or carries himself; often synonymous with pride. *My swag ain't like the world's; my swag is the thankfulness I have toward God for saving me.*

The Block—Inner-city street corners; a place for gathering, socializing, and selling drugs. *Yo, we 'bout to hit the block and preach the Gospel!*

Thebonics—The presentation of theological truths in the language known as Ebonics.

Throwback jersey—A sports jersey that was worn by re-tired professional athletes, often worn in the city for fashion. *I just got that Walter Payton throwback, son.*

Tookie Williams—Stanley "Tookie" Williams was one of the founders of the Crips gang in Los Angeles. In 1979, he was convicted of committing four murders and sentenced to death. Before his execution by lethal injection in 2005, he authored children's books and books that carried antigang messages.

Took/take the rap—To take the blame and punishment for a crime that you did not commit. The crime is then placed on the innocent person's "rap sheet" (Record of Arrest and Prosecution), listing them as the convicted criminal. *What I love about the Gospel is that it hits me off with the truth that Jesus Christ took the rap for me and now I can be free from the penalty and price of my sin.*

Weight—A replacement term for cocaine. See ***movin' weight***.

Young Money Entertainment—A record label started by rapper Lil Wayne that carries much influence with a lot of young people today. *I got only Young Money on my iPod.*

The ReBuild Initiative

For years saints in the urban context have been looking for a healthy church that has solid doctrine, biblically qualified leaders, on top of a multicultural congregation that is missionally engaged with their immediate community. A church of this description is not often found in the urban core, so many urban saints have found resolution to drive 30 to 45 minutes outside of the city to enjoy such fellowship. As the commute to the suburban church becomes burdensome, the heart of the urban saint grows more passionately in love with the urban context, leaving them to contemplate one question: why don't we have this type of church in the urban core?

A group of urban pastors began the ReBuild Initiative after they all sensed God calling them to live out 2 Timothy 2:2 by dedicating the rest of their lives multiplying urban leaders with the Gospel. The ReBuild Initiative is a network of churches (newly planted or replanted) that provide solid biblical preaching, conservative theology, and cultural relevance all demonstrated through missional engagement inside the urban context.

The ReBuild Initiative focuses on empowering, encouraging, and equipping urban pastors and leaders to serve with diligence in their city by providing for them a trusted portfolio of contextualized resources. This includes Roundtables in major North American cities; assessments that have been crafted to address and prepare the urban church planter and his family for the unique pressures they will face; and resources that address urban issues that are often not discussed outside of the urban context.

If you are interested in church planting, becoming part of the urban church conversation, or desire to partner with ReBuild, please visit http://therebuildinitiative.org/ for more information.